God's Love For You!

Study Guide

Chase Aderhold
Rudi Louw

Table of Content

1. *God Doesn't Need to Change* 5
2. *God Wants to Reveal Himself* 11
3. *God Desires Companionship* 33
4. *God's Pursuit of Us* 51
5. *God's Pursuit Frees From Alternatives* 81
6. *Abiding in the Son and in the Father* 93
7. *The Love We Have for One Another* 99

Chapter 1

God Doesn't Need to Change

I. The Affection of Christ

A. Philippians 1:8, *"I long for you all with the affection of Jesus Christ."* Paul reveals that both Jesus and the Father have very real emotions. After all they are the very source of our ability to have emotions.

B. We as human beings are not in a state of trying to win the favor of God or change the way He feels about us. Religion persuades us to try and make ourselves better people in order to become more presentable before a moody old God. But GOD DOESN'T NEED TO CHANGE!

C. All the while Man was bringing sacrifices and offerings before God in order to try and attain His favor; God spoke our law-language and prophetically revealed that He had His own Lamb in mind. Jesus appeared as the, *"Lamb of God ...that takes away the sin of the world"* (John 1:29), showing us that **it has never been Man trying to win**

God's favor, it has always been God trying to win Man's favor.

II. Peace With God

A. In realizing it's always been the unchanging God trying to change our opinions and attitudes, *it brings peace.* We must be reconciled to the fact that God's heart and mind have never changed towards us; *God has settled in His heart how He feels about us.* God is at peace with Himself and with us. God is not ruled by fickle fleeting emotions, because God is not at war with Himself or anyone. Every aspect of God's being; every attribute of God, flows from who He is in His heart. At His core, GOD IS LOVE! He's always been love!

B. 2 Peter 1:2, *"Grace and peace be multiplied to you **in the knowledge** of God our Father and the Lord Jesus Christ."* Literally: Grace and peace is multiplied to us in the Godhead's knowledge of themselves and of us, now revealed to us in the gospel Romans 5:1, *"Now we have peace with God through our Lord Jesus Christ."* How? Through their knowledge revealed to us! Being justified freely by God's faith and by God's grace. Jesus is what God believes about you! The successful work of Redemption accomplished in Jesus Christ is what God believes about the human race!

Questions

1. What does religion attempt to persuade us to do?

2. What evidence do we have to show us that God's favor never had to be won?

3. Describe in your own words how grace and peace gets multiplied to us.

4. After you have worked through the book, return to this page, and review your answer to the previous question.

Chapter 2

God Wants to Reveal Himself

I. Our Eternal Connection

A. Ephesians 1:17-18, *"...that the God of our Lord Jesus Christ, the Father of glory, may give to you the spirit of wisdom and revelation in the knowledge of Him ...the eyes of your understanding being enlightened; that you may know what is the hope of His calling..."*

B. Ephesians 1:4-5, *"He* [God] *chose (**associated**) us in Him* [in Christ] *before the foundation* (before the fall, Katabalo) *of the world* (Colossians 1:16-17; Ephesians 3:9b) *that we should be holy and without blame before Him, **in Love** ...In love having predestined us to adoption as sons, by Jesus Christ, to Himself, **according to the good pleasure of His will.**"*

C. According to the above scriptures, an intimate connection has always existed between God and Man, in Christ (in the Logos). This connection was made in the very beginning before the creation of the world as we know it, way before Adam's fall.

II. Jesus, the Blueprint Son

A. Jesus is the original Adam, **the original blueprint SON,** for whom, and by whom, and from whom and to whom, everything was created. The blueprint for all of creation can be traced back to Him. (Colossians 1:16, *"For by Him all things were created, in heaven and on earth, visible and invisible, whether thrones or dominions or rulers or authorities – all things were created through him and for him."*)

B. Because He's the blueprint Son, it means that *we were made in His image and likeness* (Genesis 1:26). Therefore, our original image and likeness *was preserved in Him,* even after Adam's fall. God refused to loose us in Adam, *because He'd already found us in Christ.* We are the ones who simply lost sight of our blueprint; of where we originated, *God never did!*

C. The word *"predestined"* as found in Ephesians 1:5 can also be defined as *pre-designed* or *preplanned,* alluding to the idea that something has already been planned in full, before the beginning of its construction. We have a beginning that cannot be measured in time. We began in a God who's outside of time, so our beginning cannot be measured in time, or at the moment of our appearance. We are not and cannot be defined by our natural existence. Just as Jesus existed long before his appearance as a Man, so do we, our origin can be traced back to the imagination of God in the eternal ages past; to the LOGOS. (Psalm 139:16).

III. Our Awesome Origin

A. 1 John 4:8, *"God is Love."* Throughout all eternity past there has existed a relationship without boundaries, an exchange of love, an intertwining and an enjoyment of total abandonment within the Godhead ...There existed a triune being of such freedom, full of beauty, love, and fullness of life, a being that we now call: God. (Proverbs 8:30)

B. In the midst of this relationship, this enjoyment of intimacy, at the very center of God, at the very center of Love Himself, we came into being. Love dreamed of companionship and we are the result of that dream. *The imagination of God is our design!*

C. Every invention, every creation, begins with an original thought, and we are God's. His imagination, thoughts, creative inspiration, and initiative find fullest expression in us. We're the result of what He dreamed and imagined. We are Love's dream, the product of His heart.

IV. Valued as Individuals

A. Love and friendship blossom in an environment of appreciation. To appreciate means *to discover, express, and communicate value.* We discover God's value of us by discovering His image and likeness engraved within our inner being. Every single one of us is a one of a kind work of art; a masterpiece! We have His fingerprints all over us; we are His handiwork, *in fact **our whole being reflects His glory.***

B. He didn't just give us his image and likeness as a whole; as a race of people called the human race. No, we carry His identity just as much as individuals, as we do when we gather together. We all share the same origin, and yet we are all unique, just like brothers and sisters of the same family, every bit as unique as our fingerprints.

C. It's a great mystery how Father could love the whole human race universally across all time, *and yet focus his love intensely, passionately, upon the individual.*

V. The Substance of Creation

A. John 1:1, *"In the beginning was the word* (the Logos) *and the word was with God* (Pros – face to face with, equal and intimate with God), *and the word was in very essence God;* (the Logos is) *the very essence of God."*

B. Though God used no preexistent physical substance to create the universe, He did use a substance called: *"the Logos."*

C. Logos is the word from which we derive our words logic and thought. However, it denotes more than just a fleeting thought. It indicates the totality of [a] thought: the motive behind it, the reasoning and development of it, and finally the expression of it. Thus the Logos is **the very expression of God's heart and all it contains.**

D. The first words in the Bible, "*In the beginning,*" are translated from the

Hebrew word, Bereshet, which can literally be translated as *"In the Head"*. From the very beginning of the book we see how God's ideas concerning creation went beyond a silent thought. It was more than a dream for His. When He created everything and then breathed and spoke humanity into existence, those thoughts were fully expressed. **We're an expression that originated from the original Logos.**

VI. Religious Constraint

A. Religion defined equals Man's efforts to try and define and know God, *who happens to live in the unseen realm of reality and cannot be seen with the naked eye.* Therefore, all religion is deeply flawed, because no matter how sincere our attempts, it remains but a mere guess, and we always inevitably come to the wrong conclusion. Through religion, we are attempting to restore a relationship with a God *whom we cannot see.* Even though we are aware of His existence, **He cannot be known unless He reveals Himself.** Religion is a stranger's way of trying to define and know God (due to the fact that we've been out of relationship with God since Adam).

B. Paul starts his conversation with the Athenians recognizing their sincerity in searching for a God who was yet unknown to them. He saw their religious attempts, even resulting in an *"Altar to the Unknown God,"* just in case all their attempts at definition fell short. He knew he had the answer *in the fact that God Himself had already came and revealed both Himself and our original design, in person, in Jesus Christ.*

VII. God's Nearness Revealed

A. Acts 17:26-27 *"And He has made from one blood* (from one man, Adam – or more accurately: from one substance, from one origin [from Christ; from the Logos])..." The word *"blood"* is not in the original manuscript, and so it should actually read, *"He has made **from One (from God Himself)** ...every individual in every nation of men to live on all the face of the earth ...that they might grope for Him and find Him, though He is not far from any one of us."* God is so near because He is the One upholding everything, even our existence, by the **word** of His power (by His Logos).

B. Religion usually excludes people from God, putting them outside of His influence and reach. However, Man is already included and revealed to be within God's embrace and under God's influence already *to some degree.*

C. Paul quoted a Philosopher and Poet named Aratus in Acts 17:28: *"...in Him we live and move and have our being..."* Aratus lived around 300 B.C., at a time when Israel's prophets were silent. Through him, God was indicating the inaccuracy, (the deafness, and blindness), as well as the dying away of the old religious system. The Law of Moses and the religious system built around it was about to be replaced as God was going to reveal the truth about Man, and reveal the truth about Himself, *in the same moment.*

VIII. Overlooking Ignorance

A. Acts 17:29, *"Therefore, since we are the offspring of God, we ought not to think that the Divine Nature is like gold or silver or stone, something shaped by art and man's devising."* God was not our invention, we were His. Therefore, we have no right to our own concepts of who He is and who we are, *because they'll always be inferior.*

B. Acts 17:30, *"Truly, these times of ignorance God overlooked, but now He commands* (based on what He did for us and on the Truth revealed by Him) *all men everywhere to repent."* The word repent is **Metanoia,** *a change of mind.* He desires us, based on the truth He has revealed, to come to different and more accurate conclusions, and thus change our opinion about Him and about ourselves, *resulting in a change of action towards ourselves and others.*

C. All the inaccurate conclusions were overlooked because the truth regarding Him and us were yet to be fully revealed. But now that He's revealed both us and Him, in the man, Christ Jesus, *we have no reason to remain ignorant;* **we have a new reference point that defines both His and our true identity.** Therefore He can call us to go through a repentance (a **Metanoia,** a **Metamorph**), *a change of thinking and being, a total metamorphosis; a change and transformation including mind, attitudes, and actions.*

IX. Judged as Righteous

A. Acts 17:31, *"...because He has appointed a day on which He **judged** the whole world, in righteousness, by the Man* (Jesus) *whom He has ordained. He has given assurance of this to all, by raising Him from the dead."* Romans 4:25, *"He was delivered up **because of** our offenses and was raised **because of** our justification; **because of** our righteousness* (because we were declared righteous ...*because our original righteousness was restored to us as a gift)."* See also Acts 10:28 and 2 Corinthians 5:14, 16.

B. The Greek in Acts 17:31 clearly indicate that Paul was referring to ***a judgment which has already taken place***. Paul began his message by declaring **God's own conclusion of our value and worth due to our origin in Him.** He established our true identity and true value (our righteousness) and brought it to a final conclusion and exclamation point in Jesus' taking our judgment upon Himself. Then He further concluded His love for us in that Jesus not only died our death, but was raised **as proof to us of our righteousness.** We now have proof that Father holds nothing against us, overlooking the times of ignorance and the results thereof.

X. Truth Revealed

A. John 4:24, *"God is spirit, and those who worship Him must worship in spirit and truth."* God's desire is that Mankind worship Him for who He truly is, from an accurate understanding of the Truth (of who we are to Him and who He is to us). *The most accurate form of worship and devotion is our spirits engaged in His truth; engaged in His Spirit ...fully engaged in His love revealed ...infatuated with Him who is love!*

B. God desires to cease remaining a mystery. That's the reason for the Bible and the Logos becoming flesh in Jesus. We even got our attributes from God; He is a lot more like us *because we are a lot more like Him than we think.* **We're wired to be like God.**

C. Even before He brought us, His perfect companion forth, from Himself, He created everything we see, *so that His heart of love for us would be revealed to us.* He expressed the attributes of His character in all of creation. It's similar to the way a man prepares gifts before he goes to present himself to his bride to be.

D. Romans 1:20-21, *"For since the creation of the world, His invisible attributes are clearly seen, being understood by the things that are made; so that they are without excuse, because, although they knew God, they did not glorify Him as God, nor were they thankful, but became futile in their thoughts, and (so) their foolish hearts became darkened."* The truth was always on display for those who look for it.

E. Psalm 19:1-4, *"The heavens declare the glory of God, and the expanse of heavens shows His handiwork. Day unto day utters speech, and night unto night reveals knowledge. There is no speech, no language* (they communicate in silence; nevertheless they are communicating, and there is no people-group, no nation) *where their voice is not heard. Their reach has gone out throughout all the earth* (they have reached the whole earth with their silent but loud message), *and their words to the ends of the world."* Creation is trying to tell us something, trying to share with us God's communication. **Creation is**

God's love letter to us.

F. Even in the Genesis account of creation, love and passion is revealed as the driving force behind it all. God stood back after creating each and every item and appreciated its detail for what it communicates to Man. He evaluated it, enjoying what He had just done. 1 Timothy 6:17, *"God gives us richly all things to enjoy."*

Questions

1. In your own words, define what it means to be associated with someone.

2. How are we defined by our association with different people?

3. How does your association with Christ define you?

4. What does Christ being the blueprint from which everything was created imply about us? Where does it say we came from and what we were designed to be?

5. *"God's imagination is your origin!"* (pg. 37, *God's Love For You*) What does that statement mean to you?

6. Does your origin in God's imagination challenge the way you see yourself? How so?

7. Think of the way coins have images and likenesses engraved upon them. When we discover God's image and likeness engraved upon us, what do we discover about ourselves and others?

8. Define the word Logos. (pg. 39, *God's Love For You*)

9. Define Religion. (pg. 42, *God's Love For You*)

10. Read John 1:17. How did God replace the Law of Moses and the religious system built around it? (Paragraph VII, Section C)

11. On what basis does God call us to repentance or (Metanoia)?

12. Define the word: Metanoia.

13. If Metamorphosis is merely a change in form as opposed to a change in nature, what are the implications, to us, of such a discovery?

14. What does Jesus' resurrection prove about us?

15. What does creation proclaim about God's love for us?

16. In Genesis Chapter 1, what seems to be the driving force behind creation?

Chapter 3

God Desires Companionship

I. The Pinnacle of Creation

A. Every part of creation was finished with the exclamation from God, *"...it is good"*, revealing that He put His heart into creation.

B. Genesis 1:27-28, 31. The pinnacle of creation was the bringing forth of Man, hence the usage of the words, *"very good"*. All things that were made before us were made for us.

C. When the Bible says, *"God blessed Man,"* the word used is the word Baw-rak, an estimation of value term which can be defined as an act of adoration such as kneeling or falling on your knees in wonder or amazement at the perfection of beauty. It is an indication of when someone is entirely overwhelmed and in awe. Mankind was *"very good"* or exceptionally enjoyable.

D. Zephaniah 3:17, *"He rejoices over us with gladness. He rests in His love. He is elated over you with singing!"*

Nothing but bringing Man forth from within Himself brought about that kind of reaction from the Father. God rejoiced in the fact that the reality of His dream finally stood in front of Him. Because of this, a companionship now exists; a constant and unending flow of friendship, fellowship, and enjoyment of life together.

II. God's Unfailing Plan

A. The word foreknew has to do with the dream in one's heart. It's similar to the way one enjoys a project before its completion, because they've already imagined and enjoyed the finished product in their minds.

B. Ephesians 1:11b, *"... [God] works all things to the counsel of His will."* God doesn't plan and fail. Everything turned out exactly in accordance to His design.

C. Deuteronomy 32:3-4

III. Called to Fellowship

A. 1 Corinthians 1:9, *"God has called us into the fellowship of His Son, Jesus Christ."* Our calling is to share in the exact same fellowship which

Jesus enjoys with the Father.

B. The word fellowship is the word Koinonia, which means friendship, communication, interaction, fun, companionship, partnership, camaraderie, intimacy, and intercourse. There's a desire in God that we alone can fulfill.

C. Even though God is perfect and needs nothing, He has desired us. He has chosen to need us because He has revealed Himself to be love (1 John 4:8). In order to be love and to love perfectly, one must open one's heart and become vulnerable.

D. In order for there to be lasting fulfillment in love, it has to be echoed. Satisfaction can come from nothing less than equal feedback.

E. Though love is more than mere emotion, true love exhibits extremely strong emotion, because it is totally engaged, with no emotional disconnect! God is relentless in His love, which is why His very name is Jealous. He's not self-absorbed and petty. He'll settle for nothing less than all of you! Sin and all lies and deception that come to steal kill and destroy in your life will be overcome and destroyed by the truth revealed in His relentless love for us!

F. Romans 2:4, *"...the goodness of God (the love of God realized and grasped) is exactly what leads us to repentance (to Metanoia)."* God's relentlessness in His love quickens and cultivates the same response of the same quality and kind within us.

IV. Brought Forth from Eternity

A. Genesis 1 26-27; 2:7. The word *Aw-saw* means to bring forth. *"Let us **bring forth** man..."* [From within ourselves].

B. Though our bodies might originate in fragility, we ourselves are so much more than dust. We are spirit beings, breathed from the very depths of God. We are not from the earth, *we are from God.*

C. Psalm 139:13-14, *"For you have formed my **inward parts** (my spirit-being, the real me); You have **covered me** in my mother's womb.* (That covering is not us, it is just the bodies we live in) *I will praise you for I am fearfully and wonderfully made."* David is not just speaking about the body we live in, he's speaking of us apart from the body.

D. We are spirit beings created to be

God's companions. Being made in His image and likeness means we were made according to His image and molded from His likeness. We are coined images, exact replicas of His image and likeness. *Not only was He the pattern and mold, but He was the origin as well!*

E. Due to the fact that Man was made in God's image and likeness, it is only logical to conclude that we would act like God, *especially before the Fall.* Adam was a mirror image of God. What was true about God was true about Adam.

V. Search for Companionship

A. Genesis 2:18, 20, 22-24. The account of Adam searching for a companion is a prophetic picture where God reveals that it is not preferable for Him [God] to be alone. We see from the story how a helper comparable and compatible to Adam (representing God) is made.

B. We see how Adam studies every species of animal on the face of the earth. He's able to accurately define them according to their true design and identity; he becomes completely familiar with them. *But among them there was no helper fit for him.* This reveals how God had more than pets in mind when He created us. He was looking for a being who was *"...bone of his bone and flesh of his flesh."*

C. We can see how everything that happened to Adam before the Fall happened as a prophetic picture pointing to God's desires. There was such a sweet fellowship between Father, Son, and Holy Spirit that was so full and pleasurable that God felt compelled to reproduce Himself and bring forth from within Himself a companion to lavish that love and fullness upon.

D. As we read on in Genesis 2, we see how God actually made us out of Himself in order for us to be a companion, just as Eve was taken out of Adam for Adam. (Acts 17:28)

VI. Bone of my Bones

A. The reality of our oneness with God and God's desire for companionship is no longer a mystery. It is actually a dominant theme in scripture, revealed by the Spirit of God. Adam's story shows us the connection that existed between God and Man since the beginning.

B. The connection between God and Man is fully reflected when we look at Christ's connection and intimate love relationship with His Bride (the Church).

C. The word Ekklesia refers to the ones who have seen, grasped, understood, embraced, entered into, and enjoy the reality of their identity and connection with God and the risen Christ.

D. The phrase used in Genesis 2:23, *"This is **now** bone of my bones and flesh of my flesh..."* is a profound prophetic statement indicating that those who embrace the reality of the love God have for us and that we come from Him experiences that very connection. We literally become Christ's Body, where He comes to dwell in all His fullness.

VII. Linked Forever

A. Just as Eve was one with Adam because she came out of Adam and yet remained inseparably linked to Adam, we too come from God and have remained inseparably linked to Him.

B. Though our association with Christ was lost in our minds, and in all practical reality in our experience, the eternal reality of it never went away. Because of that unbreakable eternal reality, Christ's resurrection was humanity's new birth. We were quickened and made alive to the love of God again, thus we were raised to newness of life in Him, in our relationship to God.

C. Romans 15:13, *"...there is joy and peace in believing."* The conclusion of what happened to humanity in Christ's death and resurrection is a faith thing from start to finish, where we begin to accept God's reality.

D. **What God believes and knows to be true about humanity *is an absolute REALITY*,** making everything *else,* every other opinion, every contrary expression that opposes that reality, a deception, a lie, an illusion, a mirage, a ruse; an un-reality.

VIII. Inheritance in Companionship

A. Genesis 2:24; 1 Corinthians 6:17. Marriage is a picture of the love-connection between God and us, reestablished in Christ.

B. Right from the beginning, God blessed Adam and Eve with

everything they needed to be happy. Enjoyment of everything they did together was their portion.

C. The fact that they were created to relate to God in the truest sense, being together was both their, as well as God's, greatest fulfillment and enjoyment and reason for life itself.

D. Because of our design for intimate companionship, we are the only beings in all of creation with the capacity to hurt, grieve, or even disappoint God.

E. However, God is not ruled by disappointment. His emotions serve Him, not the other way around. The Spirit of Truth rules in His heart. Jesus Christ the same yesterday, today and forever. In God there is no dark side, no fickleness; no variableness. He is stable in His love. Love is unchanging and unconditional and gives continually (1 Corinthians 13). Though God was devastated at the Fall and cried out in agony for the reestablishment of His intimate connection with Adam, nothing, no amount of disappointment or anything else could overrule His heart and mind in order to get Him to stop loving us.

Questions

1. What are some of the ways we can tell from the Genesis 1 account of creation that there was a lot of passion and love driving the creation of all things?

2. Define *Baw-rak*. Does that challenge your view of God? Does that challenge your view of yourself? Explain.

3. Define Koinonia as used in 1 Corinthians 1:9. Based off of this verse, can we see anyone as outsiders, utterly removed from the presence of God?

4. In order for there to be lasting fulfillment in love, it has to be _____.

5. Why is God's name Jealous (Section III, Paragraph E)?

6. What do the passages in Genesis 1:26-27, 2:7 and Psalm 139:13-14 say about the distinction between our bodies and us?

7. We're more than our bodies. We are _____ beings created to be God's _____. (Section IV, Paragraph D)

8. Why is it logical to conclude that we have the capacity to and therefore in many ways do act like God?

9. Read Genesis 2:18, 20, 22-24. How can we infer that God had more than pets in mind when He created us? What does Adam's searching for companionship say about God?

10. Adam's story shows us the connection between God and Man that has existed since the beginning. What is the full reflection of that connection in the New Testament scriptures?

11. Define Ekklesia.

12. What does the fact that Eve came out of Adam and remained linked to Adam assure us of?

13. The conclusion of what happened to humanity in Christ's death and resurrection is a _____ thing from start to finish. (Section VIII, Paragraph C)

14. What can be said about what God knows to be true? (Reality vs. Un-Reality)

15. God blessed Adam and Eve with everything they needed to be happy from the beginning. What can we say was their portion? Explain.

16. What about our design makes us the only ones who can grieve, hurt, or disappoint God? Can we ultimately actually grieve, hurt, or disappoint God?

Chapter 4

God's Pursuit of Us

I. Forbidden Unto Separation

A. Adam and Eve could eat from any tree in the garden except partake from the knowledge of good and evil. God warned them that they would die if they ate from that tree, *but He never said **He** would kill them.*

B. We can conclude from the fact that a forbidden tree was accessible in the garden that God didn't have a bunch of mindless robots in mind when He created us. *Man's choice to love God of their own free will was His desire.*

C. But that tree wasn't a test either. There were plenty of other trees to enjoy besides that one. Just as in a marriage, there were boundaries that existed with the relationship between God and Man. There was an understood separation unto each other which partaking of the fruit of that other tree would destroy.

II. Deliberate Deception

A. Adam and Eve deliberately chose to eat from that tree themselves. Eve was deceived about what God said, but Adam knew it as firsthand information. *He embraced the lie and began to question **the truth** behind what God had said.* **Adam allowed suspicion towards God's motives to enter his heart,** *causing the truth he already knew to be called into question.*

B. An ignorant person can be deceived easily, but an educated person has to deceive themselves first *before any lie can stick,* and that is where Adam's guilt lay.

C. In taking that fruit, Adam partook of the fruit of reasoning between good and evil for yourself, and thus being a god unto yourself. *But in doing so, he violated something within himself and yielded himself to the forces of darkness and death.*

D. The Tree of the Knowledge of Good and Evil *represents a partaking of an outside force and influence which gets inside of you, becoming one with you.*

E. The fall was not brought about by the partaking of that tree. Rather, it was brought about by the manipulation of

Satan (His accusation) and the embrace of the suspicion towards God because of the lie he told them.

F. Adam's partaking of the natural tree was a sign which pointed to the fact that *he already fell.* God's warning regarding that tree was exclaiming that by the time Adam ate of that tree, *he would have already believed a lie regarding God and himself,* **causing a breakdown in the relationship.**

G. Eating the fruit of that tree was actually the result of a process which unleashed deadly spiritual forces in the world which became like a virus or like cancer and left Man trapped and without escape.

III. The Illegal Contract

A. The deadly poison of what Adam had allowed in his heart caused a very real separation.

B. Satan powerfully and practically gained influence over Adam and everything under Adam's control. Adam sold himself, his wife, all of Mankind yet unborn, and the whole earth in an illegal, but binding transaction. We were sold into bondage and slavery to evil's influence, manipulation, and rule. **This became Man's practical and long term experience and reality.**

C. The Law of Sin and Death came to power under that contract, *causing the symptoms to spread like a plague and becoming firmly established.* We were trapped in the natural realm and reduced to a natural minded dimension of life. *This world became our god* (2 Corinthians 4:4).

D. We have evidence that Adam in a way gave the world over to Satan in Luke 4:5-6, when Jesus is tempted in the wilderness. ("*...I will give you all this power and authority **which has been handed over to me**...*")

E. However, though this law came into power practically, *it was not actually **legal**.* Psalm 24:1 states that, *"The earth **is the Lord's and the fullness thereof, the world and those that dwell therein**."*

IV. Guilt and Weakness

A. The power of the enemy to control the world then lies in only one thing: ***Man's Guilt.***

B. The weakness of the flesh is not a weakness in our body; it is a weakness in our thinking, *tying us to a natural mindset and existence in separation from God.*

C. This is only established and reinforced *through guilt, manipulation, and sin-consciousness* through our initial cooperation, which is how it all came into power in the first place and continues to be in power.

D. However, the enemy is only a thief. His power is weak because he used lies, manipulation, and deception to set up an illegal transaction.

E. Because the transaction is **illegal**, it means the stronghold the enemy has over Mankind is weak, and the minute he is discovered as a thief, he has to return what was stolen. *In the light of eternal truth, the control the enemy has over us loses its power and control.*

F. Jesus spoke these words from a relation to a successful work of redemption: John 12:31, *"Now shall the prince of this world be cast out."* Luke 10:18, *"I saw Satan fall like lightning from heaven."*

G. But even if Adam and Eve could re-discover the truth, **their guilt still remained intact within their hearts**

and minds. There had to be a legal transaction between them and God which would remove their guilt, legally and practically in their minds.

V. Lost Innocence and Love's Initiative

A. The Fall happened to us in our thinking, and therefore it happened in our spirit, and in our hearts and in our conduct. *We lost our innocence.*

B. However, the Fall never happened to God. God didn't fall, *we did.* And God knew that Love had to take initiative and intervene in a strong, binding way.

C. God didn't just ignore our binding reality and leave us in our bondage. He set us free to enjoy the place we originally had in Him; *the place we never truly lost.*

D. Though the Fall was an illegitimate matter concerning God, He couldn't ignore our feelings regarding it, *because what we consider legal **is practically binding upon us.*** We would have considered God unrighteous if He'd simply forgiven our sins, because we through the lie and suspicion we embraced considered God a judge.

E. God had to come and deal with our sin in a way that satisfied all the legal terms required *in Man's mind and heart.*

F. Killing us as punishment was not an option for a Father who is relating to his children. **He loved us too much** to start over with another creation.

VI. The Plan of Redemption and The Seed

A. So God promised a Seed (not many, but One Seed) through whom would come freedom and rescue from that lie and that virus of sin which was embraced and unleashed that day.

B. Genesis 3:22. God put Adam and Eve out of the Garden because of Love, *"...lest they eat also of the tree of life and remain in that fallen state forever."*

C. Redemption was not a Plan B. It was a continuation of Plan A!

D. All the names of God in the Old Testament represent a manifestation of His love towards His People, Israel, who were prophetically called His People because He'd chosen them to be the ones through whom The Seed would come which would bless the whole world.

E. Israel became God's chosen people so that all nations would be blessed through them. Now God has chosen us believers, set apart through the understanding of the Gospel and the faith it produces, to be a new holy nation through which to bless Israel in return.

F. God's election works inclusion, not exclusion. He's always had more than the individual in mind. When He wants to bless everyone, He chooses one through whom to bless.

G. Isaiah 5:1-7. There are many parables in the Old Testament pointing to the fact that the people of Israel, though chosen to be His people, were not truly His people, this was evident in their God forsaking ways. God, therefore, was going to have to reject them **as a nation** so that they could enter His kingdom **individually** through the influence of the Church, *just like the rest of Mankind, so that we all together can be His new royal priesthood and Holy Nation.*

H. Over and over, God reached out to Israel, only to be rejected. This prophetically pointed to the state of fallen Man and to the Messiah coming through them as a people.

I. God has a special place in His heart for Israel because they are the heritage of Abraham, who was His friend, and even Jesus has a body which descends from them. *He wants them to understand His heart and come into salvation through the Gospel.* Matthew 23:27.

J. But Israel was still just a prophetic picture pointing to the fact that the state of Fallen Man was getting progressively worse and needed Jesus to come as a Savior. Psalm 8:4. Isaiah 53:6. Romans 3:9-12, 23.

K. All throughout history, one can witness that the disease of sin had deeply rooted itself in humanity. It was like Satan, the accuser, was constantly crying out against us, and mocking God in His creation of us, declaring how much we didn't deserve God's love.

L. However, though God had every right to destroy Man, He'd already made up His heart and mind to love and rescue us *because of our eternal unchanging association in Christ* (Ephesians 1:4-5; Proverbs 8:30-31). He never stopped loving us because He had made up His heart and mind about us!

M. Companionship and intimacy is what God wants from us, and intimacy with God is also what we need to be fulfilled. This was the driving factor behind Jesus' death.

VII. Understanding Love's Pursuit

A. Mankind had disgraced God and violated His trust, as well as insulted His goodness and kindness towards us. We came under Satan's influence and were all living in a *Hell of our own making, co-constructed by Satan and ourselves.*

B. Though Hell is just as real as Heaven and Earth, Jesus spoke much more *about Father's love for us* than any of these other realities.

C. 1 Timothy 2:4. If we perish and end up in Hell, it will be by our own hand, because of our own unbelief, *the inevitable result of a rejection of truth.*

D. But Love never stops trying. God is absolutely convinced of His love for us and our value to Him, and will never cease trying to get our attention.

E. 1 John 5:11-12, *"God has given us eternal life, and this life is in His Son. He who has the Son has life; He who does not have the Son of God does not have life."*

F. But the issue is not about *"getting"* the Son. It's about seeing that eternal life which was manifested and then redeemed and restored to us in the Son's work of redemption. The issue has been and will always be ***understanding***.

G. Once we believe and embrace these things, Jesus and Father comes and manifests themselves in and through us, making their home in us by the Spirit of Christ, who comes to persuade us of truth (John 14:15-23).

H. As long as the law of sin and death legally stood against us in our minds and hearts, there could be no reconciliation between us and God. But God sent Jesus, putting everything on the line, laying Himself bare, *making His heart fully known*.

I. John 3:16. God went to great lengths, at enormous personal cost He demonstrated His love, *in order to redeem and rescue our minds and hearts out of darkness.*

J. Romans 5:8. God came in person to release us of our offense by saying: YOU ARE FORGIVEN, all because we in our minds as a binding reality could not justify merely ignoring it. God came on His own initiative to redeem and release us of our guilt and so called debt to Him, it is only based on that that we can muster the courage to forgive ourselves and continue in relationship with God without any guilt or shame.

K. Isiah 53:5. Ephesians 1:6; 2:8. We must focus on God's grace and goodness and stop focusing on our unworthiness.

VIII. New Covenant Reconciliation

A. Colossians 2:13 -15, *"And you, being dead in your trespasses* (in other words, still being under the law of sin and death and its enslavement) *He made alive together with Him, having forgiven you all trespasses."* God wiped out the very sin we knew and felt we had committed against Him, setting us free from the power which the law of sin and death had over our lives **by His mighty display of love.**

B. This was a totally legal action *because of our eternal and valid association with Him.* He established the New Covenant between Jesus, who represented us, and Himself in such a way that we could never mess it up!

C. In establishing the New Covenant, He actually re-established the eternal covenant between Himself and Jesus, *with us as witnesses and beneficiaries.* Now we can be reconciled on that much stronger basis.

IX. Re-Newed Righteousness

A. 2 Corinthians 5:18-21, *"God has reconciled us to Himself through Jesus Christ. God was in Christ;* (He came in person) *reconciling the world to Himself, not imputing their trespasses to them. Therefore we are ambassadors for Christ, as though God was pleading through us, we implore you on Christ's behalf, BE reconciled to God. For He made Him* (Jesus) *who knew no sin to be sin for us, that in Him* (in His work of redemption) *we might become* (not slowly over time, but instantly, through faith, be restored to) *the righteousness of God."*

B. God made a legal exchange, causing Jesus to become sin with our sinfulness **so that we could become righteous with His (and our *original*) righteousness.**

C. Colossians 1:12-14, *"God the Father has qualified us to be partakers of the inheritance of the saints **in the light*** (in the light of truth; we become saints, or set apart ones, or purified ones, when we embrace God's light; when we believe God's truth). *He has delivered us from the power of darkness* (or ignorance and deception)*; and translated us into the kingdom of* (Christ) *the son of His love. In Him we have redemption through His blood; we* (already) *have the forgiveness of sins."*

D. Redemption can be defined as a price which was paid, to purchase or buy back out from under the influence and control of. It speaks of a releasing on receipt of ransom, to release by paying a ransom price. It is used to describe both the release from the consequences of transgression and a release from the transgression itself. It also refers to buying up an opportunity or making the most of every opportunity and turning it to the best advantage.

E. Redemption does not mean that Jesus came to negotiate with God the angry judge for our release and to buy us back out of His hand. Redemption also does not mean that

Jesus came to pay a ransom price to Satan to buy us back out of his hands. God didn't need to come and negotiate with Satan for our release. He owed Satan nothing because no matter how long a thief has something in their possession, it never actually becomes theirs.

F. Also, God didn't try and pay the lowest possible price in order to buy back a used up humanity. No! In the price He was prepared to pay, He was dealing with us! He had to rescue our minds from darkness; He had to buy us back out of the hands of ignorance! *He had to convince us of our worth and value to Him.*

G. Thus, without even dealing directly with Satan, He completely defeated Satan (the voice of accusation) by the transaction He made with us, in the open display of His eternal love for us, *exposing the devil and all his lies.* The devil was openly rebuked and put on public display; he has made a spectacle **when God revealed His own love for us and canceled our debt, proving to us that we are of the highest value to Him (still).**

H. God dealt so thoroughly with our debt and sin that he could totally remove it not only from His own mind, but from ours, so neither we nor He may ever remember it again. *In time* He came in person and dealt so thoroughly with our sin and forgave us and thus proved that we stand forgiven.

I. However, *in eternity* **it has always been a reality.** Even throughout all the ages past in the prophetic deceleration of the Scriptures *God declared that it was already done. Our sins were already forgiven.* He revealed that He already forgave us *before the fall ever happened.* He had already seen the end from the beginning **and chose not to hold anything against us.** Hence, in His mind and heart, *"the Lamb (Jesus) was slain from before the foundation of the world."*

J. The fact that God never stopped loving us and overlooked the times of ignorance *is an eternal reality.* The price He paid to redeem us was *to* us, **in order to convince us of this reality, the reality of His eternal love for us!**

X. The Display of the Cross

A. He rescued our minds and hearts from strongholds of darkness, lies, deception, ignorance, sin, guilt, and condemnation, *in the work of redemption,* giving us a seasonable time and opportunity to believe His love and embrace the work of salvation and be reconciled to Him.

B. The cross does not satisfy the anger of God, but rather is holy love. Jesus' *self*-sacrifice reveals that God is not the bloodthirsty Deity we believed Him to be. It was actually humanity that was bloodthirsty.

C. An angry and vengeful God did not make the cross necessary. It wasn't a payment to satisfy a God who is bound by a sense of justice and demands blood.

D. The wrong idea we held where God is a judge who can't get over our sin *was replaced* by the revelation that **God is a father who simply can't get over His kids.** God is our Daddy who loves us. It was Him who took the initiative to identify with us to the uttermost. *The cross was the entire Godhead's* **undignified public display of affection towards Mankind,** *just to win our hearts in love and get us to return to His bosom again!*

Questions

1. If the presence of the Tree of the Knowledge of Good and Evil wasn't a test, what was it?

2. Eve was deceived about what God said, but what did Adam begin to question?

3. What does the Tree of the Knowledge of Good and Evil represent? What did the natural tree (of the Knowledge of Good and Evil) point to? What would have already happened by the time Adam ate of its fruit?

4. After the Fall, what became Mankind's practical reality? What Law came into power after that?

5. How do we know that this Law was not actually legal?

6. Where did/does the enemy's power over us lie?

7. Define the weakness of the flesh.

8. The Fall was an illegitimate matter concerning God, but He couldn't just ignore our feelings regarding it. Why? How did we need God to respond?

9. Why was wiping Mankind off the face of the earth and starting over not an option?

10. Why did God put Adam and Eve out of the Garden?

11. What was God's motive behind choosing Israel as His people?

12. What does God's election look like? Exclusion or Inclusion?

13. Why does God have a special place in His heart for the Israeli people?

14. What were Israel and their constant rejection of God a prophetic picture of?

15. _____ and _____ is what God wants from Man, and _____ with God is what we need to be fulfilled (Section VI, Paragraph M)

16. What did Jesus speak about more than the realities of Heaven and Hell?

17. Read 1 John 5:11-12. What's the point of that verse? What should we understand regarding the work of redemption?

18. Why did God show up personally to forgive us of our offense?

19. Why was it now legal for God to wipe out our sin?

20. Who is the New Covenant established between? Why is it now impossible for us to mess it up?

21. Define the word: Redemption.

22. Who did Jesus come to negotiate with in the work of Redemption? God, Satan or Mankind? Why?

23. What does the price God paid say about our value to Him?

24. How did God defeat the devil in dealing with us?

25. What does the cross satisfy if not the anger of God?

26. What wrong idea was replaced in the action taken on the cross?

Chapter 5

God's Pursuit Frees From Alternatives

I. Deceptive Alternatives

A. 2 Corinthians 5:20,*"We implore you, on Christ's behalf, as though God were pleading through us, be reconciled to God."* Paul was writing to people who had already heard the gospel and yet it seemed deception was already beginning to set in and make another, lesser life, more attractive.

B. Letting a mere, natural minded identity rule your life will lull you to sleep spiritually and trap you in a lesser experience and expression of life.

C. This natural world, as well as man-made religion and wrong thinking will cause you to lose track of the truth, causing you to slip back into works or to even fall out of love with God. Religion is a poor replacement for a genuine intimate relationship.

D. Without the reality of Love sustaining

you, you die inside and begin to live a hollow shell of a life, leading you back to a life of addiction to the flesh.

II. Fullness in Relationship

A. Relationship without intimate companionship is empty. The whole purpose of relationship is intimate friendship and fellowship.

B. Jeremiah 24:7. God wants us to start embracing His truth and love while resisting Satan and religion with its lies and empty deception.

C. God didn't lower His standards of godliness or change His design of us when Jesus came and died for our sins. There was no vision for a compromised standard of design for us, or a lesser life than what we were originally designed for.

D. Our original blueprint design is about living life to the fullest together with God and giving expression to the love relationship we enjoy with Him.

E. Sin is unacceptable because it is a destructive delusion – living life in self-destruct mode. God knows the truth about us and cannot be fooled by a fake alternative to reality. The blood of Jesus doesn't mean that God now conveniently overlooks sin or that what was previously unacceptable is now acceptable. Sin is sin, it is destructive in nature. However, sin doesn't offend God. Sin causes damage to us *not God,* that's why He wants it out of our lives, and not because He is somehow offended by it Himself.

III. Designed for Fullness

A. God has revealed the truth about us and our design, and anything outside of that design is a deception. Living any kind of inferior life to that design is not what He had in mind when He designed us.

B. Redemption is not God's cop-out; it is Him restoring Man back to his original design of enjoying life together with God! We weren't designed for sin, but instead for fullness of relationship with God.

C. God wants us to fall in love with Him as much as He has always been in love with us. He desires for His initiative to quicken a quality response of love and devotion from our hearts towards Him.

D. An idol is any alternative that tries to take God's place, taking away the allegiance and devotion of our hearts to Him. This includes Man-made religious ideas.

IV. Treasured Focus

A. Jesus in His teachings always brought everything back to the focus of our hearts. We are called to treasure God's authentic truth and love.

B. Luke 8:14. The seed that fell among the thorns represent those who hear the Word of God but choke themselves with worries, riches, and pleasures of this world. *Their relationship with God is never allowed to blossom into a full-blown love affair with Him because His truth and love is not embraced and treasured as it should be.*

C. Matthew 6:19-33. Jesus was speaking about the influence of either the truth, or the deception that we focus on. Our lives, conduct, and experience, *will follow the focus and devotion of the heart* and we will never be able to divide our devotion.

D. Pursuing alternative fulfillment, even in things which cannot possibly satisfy, is a pursuit of sin. It's missing the mark; *it's outside of our original true design.*

E. *The pursuit of sin is driven by emptiness,* and that self-destructing war raging within us, that conflict of interest in our hearts can't be resolved *until we grasp the truth of our origin and our redemption and reconciliation to God our true Father.*

F. Faith, an intimate fellowship with God in the truth, is the only thing that causes us to actually be able to make the shift in our hearts and minds to be able to walk in true friendship with God.

G. Matthew 6:25-33. Undivided attention is crucial when developing and maintaining our persuasion and intimacy in the truth. When we realize that God truly and perfectly loves us, He captures our gaze and then we automatically knows that He is trustworthy to provide everything we need and all fear is driven from our hearts.

H. Matthew 7:13-14. The gospel brings us into a single-minded focus when it comes to treasuring God's truth and love in our hearts. People, who become confused about the gospel, remain messed up in their beliefs and make wrong choices because they can't help but continue in the wrong pursuits.

I. It takes genuine revelation into God's truth and love to discover a way of living without distractions. *Our value and worth was established and forever settled in God's heart.* **It's revealed in the price God was willing to pay to prove His love.**

J. Proverbs 23:4-5. 1 Timothy 6:6-11. Being content with being Father's child and living life with Him and acting like Him are true riches.

K. James 3:16; 4:1-5. Outside of God's love reigning and finding expression in us, what do we really possess? There is nothing else truly worth living for. When we pursue after empty things, we end up drifting away and resisting and opposing everything good that God desires for us.

L. It is only the knowledge of truth and our Father's love which can set us free, causing us to embrace the fact that we've been delivered from the power of darkness. Correctly understanding God's love for us causes us to know we cannot abuse it. Cherishing that intimate love relationship with Him will reveal to us and make it plain that we do not have to tolerate any empty pursuit of alternatives.

V. Casual Callousness

A. Romans 6:1-2. Living in sin with a casual attitude toward God's love is detestable indeed. It is living life in a dangerous self-destruct mode. It not only harms you but others.

B. Revelation 3:15-20. Laodecia had developed this wrong attitude due to deception and turned their Christianity into something toxic that makes everyone who comes into contact with it sick, including God. Not even God can palate such a thing! Jesus encourages them to have faith and a heart full of devotion (gold refined in the fire).

C. Repentance or Metanoia, means to come to such a revelation of the truth that it radically changes your mind. This allows you to experience a metamorphosis, a total transformation in your life and relationship with God to where you come into true Koinonia, or fellowship, with God and others in genuine, pure love.

D. 1 Corinthians 6:15, 18-20. The intimacy between a married man and woman reflects the intimacy between Christ and the Church, and this depth of intimacy is falsely imitated and therefore obscured and cheapened with the sins of homosexuality and fornication. What is experienced naturally in the intimacy of marriage between a man and a woman, that baby that comes forth in that union is a prophetic picture, pointing to the spiritual intimacy and union we enjoy with God, as well as the fruit we begin to bear as a result of it. Like marriage, between one man and one women, such intimacy is not entered into casually, nor is it considered available and open to outsiders (idols, sins, etc. - 1 Corinthians 10:21 & 22).

E. Hebrews 12:14; 2:3. Galatians 5:1. 2 Corinthians 7:1 in the Aramaic Bible in Plain English says, *"Therefore, because we have these promises made reality, beloved, let us purify ourselves from all impurity of the flesh and spirit, let us cultivate holiness in our awe of God."*

Questions

1. What happens when you let a natural minded identity rule your life?

2. What is the only thing that can sustain us, and keep us from dying inside, leaving us to fall back into a life of addiction to the flesh?

3. Relationship is empty when it lacks **what**? What is the purpose of relationship?

4. Why is sin unacceptable to God?

5. Is redemption God's cop-out? What evidence do we have that we were not designed for sin?

6. What is an idol?

7. What will we never be able to successfully divide? How can we define sin in light of pursuing alternative fulfillment?

8. What does it take in order to discover a way of living without distractions?

9. Think about what was stated earlier, *"We weren't designed for sin."* What about living in sin with a casual attitude toward God's love is so dangerous and detestable that not even God can stomach it?

10. How does Paul relate the message that intimacy with God is not to be entered into lightly in 1 Corinthians 6:15, 18-20?

Chapter 6

Abiding in the Son and in the Father

I. Responding in Repentance

A. 1 John 5:18-21. The only appropriate response to God's revelation of the truth is Repentance, or Metanoia – a change of mind about us, God, and others. The knowledge that our true identity is found in God's image and likeness fuels change in our behavior.

B. 2 Corinthians 7:1. 1 John 3:3. Romans 8:1. 1 John 2:1.

C. Jesus, as our advocate, is not up in heaven defending our wrong actions before the Father. His advocacy is to our benefit. The only case He's arguing is before you, convincing you of the truth of who you really are.

D. God's not fooling Himself; He is living by a greater truth regarding you. His mind is filled with the reality of the New Covenant – you're His child. He calls us to live in that reality as well.

II. Consistent Freedom

A. The only way to stay consistent in freedom is to have our minds and hearts filled with the same realities as God does about us.

B. 1 John 2:6. Those who set their heart on believing, embracing, and practicing the truth abide in God as a reality.

C. 1 John 2:24. 1 Corinthians 11:2. Ephesians 5:25-27. In light of what's been preached and revealed to us concerning our restoration to intimate fellowship with God, we no longer need to disappoint ourselves.

D. We are disappointed when our idols, our inferior pursuits after pleasures, leave us empty. True fulfillment is found in intimate companionship with God.

E. Ephesians 6:23-24. God trusts us with His heart, satisfaction, fulfillment, deepest emotions, and friendship.

F. Focusing on religious do's and don'ts only keep our eyes focused on us. Sin-consciousness is about focusing on what one did wrong or should have done or should be doing. In light of this inferior focus, this inferior religious relationship with God, *God's desire for true intimate friendship and fellowship with us will go unmet.*

G. Hebrews 10:38. Sin-consciousness causes us to automatically draw away from God, even while we desire and are trying to draw near to Him.

H. Ephesians 1:6; 2:4. Ephesians 3:18-19. Though your head may grow tired of 1+1=2, your heart never stops desiring to hear, *"I love you."*

I. Romans 15:13. 1 John 1:2; 4:16, 19. This life and love is a heart thing, not a head thing.

Questions

1. What is the only appropriate response to God's revelation of truth?

2. What case is Jesus, as our advocate, arguing?

3. What is the only way to stay consistently free?

4. What is the inevitable result of sin-consciousness?

Chapter 7

The Love We Have for One Another

I. Enjoyment in Equality

A. Philippians 2:5-9. God's identity was not robbed by Jesus' enjoyment of equality with Him. The Father likes it when we are imitators of Him.

B. In becoming Man, laying aside His privileges as God, God still remained God. In essence, He remained the God who is love.

C. John 13. God humbled Himself and became Man's servant, and yet was not reduced in person or dignity.

D. We can see how the incarnation and ascension are totally related because God humbled Himself and the Son of God became the Son of Man so that the Sons of Man might again be restored to the be the sons of God. The ascension is the glorification of both Jesus and Mankind.

E. In honoring Jesus, God also honored

and restored us to our original place and position of glory. Even as God became man without ceasing to be God, so we have been inseparably united with God without ceasing to be humans. We are not consumed by union and equality with God but we're released to be our true selves. We become full of love and full of God's Spirit and power.

F. Pride ceases to be an issue for those who are secure in the knowledge of who they are to their God. Being humble enough to serve is not beneath them, but becomes their joy because such deeds of love and service confirm their unchanging character of their true identity.

II. Fellowship in a Life of Love

A. John 15:12, *"This is my commandment, that you love one another just as I have loved you. This I command you, that you love one another."* God demonstrated and Jesus gave us a new mode of living, calling us to love one another. **Authentic life can only be found and lived in the love of God.**

B. The context of family is what we were designed to live in. God, as a Father, is building His family.

Therefore, Christianity is all about friendship, and intimate relationship.

C. **Love and life only thrive in the context of true friendship and family.** *Authentic life can only be lived in harmony with others.*

D. Matthew 6:43-48. Love others because the life of love is the only authentic life you can now live. You can no longer deny yourself the pleasure of living that life.

E. In the same way God came at great personal cost to restore our relationship to Him, so we should go out of our way to restore relationship with others. *Giving and generosity is the hallmark of love!*

F. If the enemy can get you isolated, your progress in the full appropriation of the truth and love in your life can become stunted. Many of our good, God given qualities cannot be developed or appropriated in isolation.

G. Philemon 1:6. We need friendship and fellowship with other believers. We're all immersed by one Spirit into one family, the family of God, the body of Christ.

H. Galatians 6:10. When we become

believers, we enter into the family of God, becoming a member of the household of faith.

I. The Christian faith is a *"together"* faith. The Holy Spirit brings us into fellowship with our Father, but also with each other.

J. 1 Peter 4:8. Ephesians 4:32. Colossians 3:12-13. Our Father's design for us is love and forgiveness *because that's who He is.* We're created in His image and likeness *and are therefore love.* **Love loves to forgive!**

III. Love's Revelation of Greater Pleasures

A. God's love is not a weak, wishy-washy thing. To love someone does not mean to accept their sin. That is an inferior representation of God's love. We are to love people out of the sin that destroys their lives.

B. Authentic love always reveals the truth of redemption and of the love of God and our freedom to give expression to our original design and true identity.

C. James 5:19-20. Galatians 6:1-2. 1 Corinthians 13.

D. Romans 12:1-2. Transformation is a metamorphosis, like the changing of a caterpillar into a butterfly. The caterpillar was always a butterfly in disguise. Its true nature came forth in the metamorphosis! James 1:18. John 8:36.

Questions

1. Read Philippians 2:5-9. What evidence do we have that God takes pleasure in our desiring a fellowship in equality?

2. How can we see how the incarnation and ascension are totally related?

3. In honoring Jesus, what did God also do?

4. What is the new mode of living that God demonstrated and Jesus gave us?

5. Only in which environment can love and life thrive?

6. What kind of faith is the Christian faith? Together or individual? How do we need one another?

7. What evidence do we have that our Father's design for us is love and forgiveness?

8. Why is accepting someone's sin an inferior representation of God's love?

9. According to Philemon 1:6 what will make our participation in the faith effective?

10. In your own words describe some practical ways to love your enemies, and get other people to open their hearts to the gospel?

www.ingramcontent.com/pod-product-compliance
Lightning Source LLC
Chambersburg PA
CBHW070523030426
42337CB00016B/2081